NEW MONKEY

Stevie Krayer

indigo dreams poetry

Indigo Dreams Publishing

First Edition: New Monkey

First published in Great Britain in 2014 by:
Indigo Dreams Publishing
24, Forest Houses
Cookworthy Moor
Halwill
Beaworthy
Devon
EX21 5UU

www.indigodreams.co.uk

ISBN 978-1-909357-47-1

British Library Cataloguing in Publication Data. A CIP record for this book can be obtained from the British Library.

Designed and typeset in Palatino Linotype by Indigo Dreams.
Cover design by Ronnie Goodyer at Indigo Dreams.
Cover painting 'The Merry Jesters' by Henri Rousseau.
Printed and bound in Great Britain by Imprint Academic, Exeter.

Papers used by Indigo Dreams are recyclable products made from wood grown in sustainable forests following the guidance of the Forest Stewardship Council.

For Seren, Rosie, Daisy and Florence

Acknowledgements

Some of these poems have previously been published in the following: *Acumen, Fragments from the Dark (anthology, Hafan Books), French Literary Review, Friends Quarterly, New Welsh Review, Jewish Quarterly, Poetry Salzburg Review, Poetry Wales, Quaker Monthly, Rialto, Running Before the Wind (anthology, Grey Hen Press), Scintilla 16 and 17.*

Three of the poems in the *Facts on the ground* sequence originally appeared in my collection *Questioning the Comet.*

Previous Poetry Publications

The Book of Hours by R M Rilke (translation),
University of Salzburg, 1994.
Voices from a Burning Boat, University of Salzburg, 1997.
Questioning the Comet, Gomer Press, 2004.
A Speaking Silence: Quaker poets of today (co-editor with
R V Bailey), Indigo Dreams Publishing, 2013.

CONTENTS

Where do we come from?

What are we?

Where are we going?

NEW MONKEY

Where do we come from?

Who has turned us around like this so that,
no matter what we do, we're in the posture
of someone who is leaving?

R M Rilke

Once upon a time in the East

A classic scene: deserted
dirt main street, wooden sidewalks,
whicker of a drowsy horse.
You'd swear you heard that lonesome
tumbleweed arpeggio
(in this case played
on a balalaika). Suddenly

a crested coach clatters into view,
scatters hens and dust, sets
the dogs barking, sweeps to a halt
at my grandparents' porch.
A closed carriage, no doubt
to protect the precious textiles
not the tailors. Still, I'm sure

the Great Ones had a soft spot
for *our Jews* – a kind of clever pet,
valuable, like hunting dogs
allowed in the house, though not
to put paws on the table.
Nor were the little tailors
intimidated by grandeur.

For Moishe was intimate
with my lord's inside leg, and Masha
had seen my lady's naked flesh
bulging over her stays
like a snow cornice. They handled
richesse every day: brocade,
silk velvet, cashmere, Brussels lace.

It was they who'd keep
a self-respecting distance, armed
with shears and chalk blade,

a battery of pins bristling
from tightened lips. Rightly, they'd
distrust the bosses' overtures, stay free
to radicalise below stairs.

My own private Bletchley Park

I had the word-cache of a bookish child
and loved to flash my ammo – only
on paper, though. Words were UXBs
liable to blow up in your face.

Yet I knew I was right. No, not a chimera
but a bewitching *shimmera*! Say *spirral*
and hear spindrift whirr and glitter!
Leave the grownups *dis-heavelled*!

Incoherent with its left-right-left-right
was far too well drilled to mean
what it said. *Incóherent,* as it should,
stumbled over itself into silence.

Home words were dangerous, too –
keep them behind closed doors.
Schissel tchannik huckmesser
not for wielding in public.

I thought they were our private lingo
till one day in the playground
a girl having birthday bumps cried
Ow, my tuchus!

It was years before
I found out my Nana's *spetchler*
was respectably English and could
stir Christmas pud as well as kugel.

But words on playground walls
were *too* goyish, couldn't be taken home.
You had to be discreet, like the side of a bus:
Shhh.... you know what.

Flesh of her flesh

She always undressed for bed
with her back to the mirror.
Naked, she still wore scars
left by the brutal
underwear that jailed her:
deep-bitten firebreaks of red
in her shoulders, whalebone striations
down buttocks and hips,
a thick stripe like a whipmark
girding her back.

Only at bedtime did she cease
to punish her flesh. Out on parole,
breasts her mother had made her strap
flat now billowed down
to a ruined belly. I stared
hard at the devastation.
In those days I still thought
the hollow of her navel
was the unclosable wound
I'd left by being born.

Friday night

We never called it Shabbat
or lit candles, but my mother's hands
dispensed praise and blessings,
smoothing the tablecloth, laying out
mosaics and pyramids and cascades
of food. Twenty dishes, displayed
as if they were jewels – olives, pearl onions,
circlets of sliced cucumber, each piled
by itself in a crystal lattice;
herrings in leaves of green glass
(shot silk the schmaltz, while the pickled
wore silver-blue lamé), fanned slices
of challah soft as an open rose.

I was allowed behind the scenes, watcher
in the scullery as she wrought
these treasures. I'd seen the original
snot-pile of raw chopped fish
that would alchemize to copper
in her alembic of molten oil, leaving
a frill of dross. The satin cream cheese
had been curds that hung all week
in a cloth over the kitchen sink,
bulging like a baby's skull, stinking
like a nappy. And khren, royally carmine,
was only beetroot juice and horseradish -
a bitter burn in the nose.

Though I knew all this, and other
secrets too – the final demands
that glowered red behind the clock,
the rotten plaster that skittered
like mice in the walls, how we took turns
to wash in the kitchen where it was warm
and because a bath cost sixpence; though Grandpa

and Dad were arguing about Stalin, their open
mouths messy with chopped liver; though
my brother was bashing his spoon
into his creamed rice so it flew, though
nothing was left of her Fabergé feast
but rubble, though I was much too young

to name it, it was festival.

Hot line

Like undertakers in their black
overcoats, handsets were weighty
portents of bad news. On the other hand,
tuppence bought you hours
of *his* voice when you were meant
to be doing your maths homework.
The family pretended not to listen.

Exchanges were human then.
They even had names –
Trafalgar, Gulliver, Museum,
Mulberry, Primrose, Scott.
Public phones, with buttons
A and B, sat in red sentry-boxes
solid enough to survive a nuclear blast.

As sabres rattled over the Caribbean
I slipped out to the high street phone-box
for a more private discussion: *Shouldn't we*
have sex, just in case?
                                        And in four minutes, how to
say goodbyes? No texting then. In the end
Krushchev blinked, pressed button B.
But who says kids think they're immortal?

War effort

A soldier lies in a hospital bed
in a hospital gown (they've taken away
his paybook and Woodbines).
He's Everyman, but for the unique
pattern of shrapnel that enamels
his young skin, the pieces missing
from his jigsawed skull, the gullet
all but cut, groin splintered.
He's still breathing. His whole being
straining towards the light.

It was your war effort. It took everything
you and the doctors together could come up with.

A diamond wedding later,
a man lies in a hospital bed
in a hospital gown (they've taken
out his false teeth). Everyman,
his mouth is that slack black yawn
eyes slide away from. Anthracite specks
still pattern his sagging skin
along with liver spots. Against his will
he's still breathing. His whole being
straining towards the dark.

But this time no-one will work with you.
You'll have to do it on your own.

23.10.43 Patient conscious, quite rational and with memory of the injury....(1) Penetrating wound over left supra-orbital region, brain tissue protruding from wound. Skin excision enlarged, one bone fragment, approximately 1.5 cm x 1.5 cm, found to be in-driven, but loose, elevated and removed, dura torn. Several smaller bone fragments also removed. Skin edges freshened. (2) Small, penetrating, sucking wound in mid-line of neck, anteriorly, explored and found to lead into the trachea. The breach in the trachea was quite large and several detached portions of cartilage were removed, tracheotomy tube left in situ. (3) Multiple small pepperings of the following places: Anterior chest wall, anterior abdominal wall, glans penis, scrotum, both thighs and both legs. All these wounds cleaned, two foreign bodies removed. Evacuate, Head Centre, lying, airlift if possible, priority 1.

26.8.55 PENSION ASSESSMENT APPEAL: Report by Neuropsychiatrist Since last Medical Board, 12th July, 1951, he states his condition has not improved. Headaches, varying types ... Longest period free of headaches is 7-10 days. Vary in severity. Still tires very easily. Sleep varies. Hard to 'get off'. Occasional depression, does not last long. Memory variable. Concentration is limited at times... Can cope with his job. Married, 2 children. Happy home but occasional difficulties due to his irritability. Few activities..... Gives good account of himself. Rational and coherent. Orientated. Attention sustained. Not depressed. Not retarded. Very slightly tense but well controlled. Seems to have adjusted now and to be living his (restricted) life on a fairly even keel.

My glamorous scarfaced dancer-Daddy,
glossy with Brylcreem, dark-suited
and burberried for the daily sorties
to that place of mysteries, Work;
domestic god, smoke-wreathed, who
sometimes romped and sometimes
raged and sometimes did my sums
in a twinkling, and sometimes
stayed frighteningly
silent and ashen, had long dwindled

in my narrowed gaze
to a clownish Polonius. How I cringed

as he buttonholed strangers, schmoozed
with waiters and waitresses – especially
waitresses – or when he shuffled in
first thing in the morning, da-daing
the Conga for attention ... even now
that he is Everyman, even while his glare
pleads for rescue like the headlamps
of a drowned submarine, while his fierce hands
struggle with the strangling kelp
of tubes, tapes, lines

I'm failing to
break through

15 November 2004. When your father came into hospital he was very sick indeed. We knew what the underlying problem was of course and that the prognosis whatever we did was poor. In hindsight deciding to put a pacemaker in was not appropriate.... As you say a diamorphine pump was not started at an early stage in fact some diazepam and then a drug called haloperidol was given on two occasions. Haloperidol is often used to settle patients with an acute confusional state secondary to other illness.... I cannot really give you a reason why nobody phoned me until late on Sunday evening and also why the diamorphine pump was left so long. I think one of the problems with acute hospital care is that our energies are put into sustaining life and we are really not as good as we should be when it comes to terminal care.

Candyfloss

It all comes back to me, queuing
for candyfloss to please
my granddaughters: in one ear

the motorbikes revving
for the Wall of Death;
in the other

the seedy wheeze
and boom as the kiddies'
roundabout restarts its ditty.

Our girls' faces, fixed
in huge identical smiles
come round and leave again

and again and again
like an overused memory
and my hands remember spinning

that useless steering wheel
connected to nothing
while the known figures slipped past.

I am back half a century
and half as tall, dumbstruck
looking up at the candy spinners:

Like mediums conjuring ectoplasm
from the sugar-spirit world
they layer up a pink nimbus

till it's piled high and wide
enough to satisfy professional pride
and a wide-eyed child.

In those days I wouldn't have
noticed they were a mother
and son, felt them as marooned

up there behind the counter in
a sweltering tin box, spotted
how she stole a moment

to look at her watch,
how she muttered to him:
Two hours to go.

Crossing

1966: here's the old Severn Princess
at the jetty. And already, see
in the background Gog and Magog
squaring up to step over no man's sea
in one contemptuous stride.
(The even airier jeté was far
in the future – *cerdd dant*
with four Aeolian harps
above a milli-legged conga line.)

Then, you had to deal nose to nose
with danger, breasting vast tides
in a Popeye boat that somehow crawled
accurately across, a flea on a silverback,
dodging the rips and shoals.
You chanced it, waiting an age
in queues, sometimes to hear
Sorry, the tide's against us. Man
had to submit (or go via Gloucester).

Mini, Anglia, Hillman Imp – all
the small fry of the small roads of the sixties –
wait their turn: that last twirl
on the Princess's wind-up gramophone
and off she sends them, away and lost
forever behind blindsiding hills.
She doesn't wait to see them pass
though her hawse-holes are already bleared
with a weep of premonitory rust.

Cerdd dant: Welsh musical form consisting of a vocal improvisation sung over a traditional melody played on the harp.

Moulin de Richard de Bas

A medieval water-driven papermill in the Auvergne

All in the one chamber, apprentice,
journeyman, master and family
would curl in their box-beds each midnight,
unborn, lulled by the muffled rhythm
of the mill's reliable heartbeat.

Close to, it's brutal: no mother's lubdub
but great nailed oaken fists, pounding
iambs and dactyls in a pentameter
of granite cisterns, battering shirt and bandage
sheet and chemise to a white gruel.

Next door, the poem emerges: a shallow form
is dipped in whitewash; one gentle shuttle
and it's settled, transmuted, looms
like developed film; is deftly turned out
on to felt – is a single sheet of paper.

Still more than half water, it must yet
be drained and pressed of superfluity
and left to season. At last, each millimetre
minutely inspected for faults, fuzziness,
hanging threads, it passes.

Complete now, linen reincarnate, it speaks
for itself in weave and watermark.
Why sully it with ink?

The doctor

The doctor by Sir Luke Fildes, Tate Gallery
[After U A Fanthorpe]

... though actually, for all his dominance
and being so brightly lit, the doctor isn't
what matters most, but what's half-hidden

in shadow: the father, standing at attention,
lumpy hand laid with care
on the slump of his wife's shoulder.

Her head's buried; his sidelong eyes
avoid the unconscious child, instead
watch the doctor watching, stymied.

The two unmatching hard chairs
that make up the sickbed, shawls
for sheets, a grown-up's discoloured pillows

tell you that somewhere out of sight
is the bed all the children
normally share. There's just the one lamp.

Dawn will soon assay all their efforts – the linctus,
the glass of wildflowers, the linnet's song,
the line of cloths, washed and washed to grey.

Close the window

Wife to husband: "Close the window, it's cold outside."
Husband: "And if I close the window, will that make it warmer outside?"
Hoary Jewish joke

Close the window, Janek –
it's cold outside, and I don't like
to hear the small voices
of the children crying.

Close the curtains, Marya –
it upsets me
to see the children shiver.
We can't help the weather.

Padlock the door, Riszard –
there's a storm raging,
but we're still safe and warm
though the house is shaking.

Close your ears, Klara –
you're better off not hearing
the children
not crying any more.

Close the book, children,
as carefully as you can.
Nothing left but names:
don't cry or the ink will run.

Ozymandias in Normandy

As we climbed on, the great propellers
began to slice the rain-sagged air
with a drone like a distant Luftwaffe
revving up for the next bomb-run.

For all their soaring, these birds
are grounded – forever doomed to circle
their hill-high turbines, great unnatural tri-limbs
flailing and moaning atop bone pillars.

Beneath them, burrowing into the slope,
a concrete blockhouse: ventilator shafts, two
oblong doorways opening into the dark.
A path gobbled by grass and nettles.

In bas-relief a grandiose headless eagle
grips a defaced globe. Square lettering
still partly readable: **IM KAMPF GEGEN ...**
ENGLAN ... Then: **.....F ..ITLER.**

Jour J 2012

June. Drone
of an engine
amplified
by hills. Not

a plane; tractor
in sunshine twirling
hay two-handed
to tidy cornrows.

Behind
hear phantom
bomb-blasts, see counter-
offensive absurdities:

haybales and cows
flying, ancient pines
turned matchwood, pastures
become craters.

Granite walls ripped
like flesh. A child
spattered
with his mother.

Such pretty names
they had for weapons:
mitraillette; flingue;
obus – shell.

Hedgerows meant
enemies. Today
they're vanishing – enemies
to prairie farmers.

Fields are smoothed
over. Even the old boy
with bits of his mum
still clinging to him

will soon be gone.
The future is picking
its way
over our oblivion

like the Normande
who stole at daybreak
across the sprawled legs
of fifty dog-tired soldaten.

What are we?

...and the resourceful animals soon notice
that we don't always feel at home
in the interpreted world.

R M Rilke

Facts on the ground

1

Today Wales has been spirited away
by fog, like that Mabinogi story
where the king and queen awake
to nothingness – court, courtiers,
fields of barley, sheep, pigs, peasants,
steam from horses, smoke from hearths,
all uncreated as if genesis
had gone into reverse. Even
the nearest trees look insubstantial

As his olive groves that aren't
there any more must look
to a Palestinian farmer
on the wrong side
of the bored boy with the Uzi.

2

Hebron

Names lose their meanings. A sign says *bridge*
or points the way. But there is no way.
Only ditches. Road blocks. Boulders. Mounds
of orange earth that gag the mouths of side-roads.
Barbed wire. Razor wire. Gun man's land. Fences.
Wire fences. Concrete fences. The Fence that is a wall.

There are gates. But gates are not gateways
until the guard says so. The road goes on –
you don't. There's a railed barrier. A striped bar.
A turnstile. A sentry-box. A guard tower.
Or just a doe-eyed girl in a booth,
her face locked tight by suspicion.

The conscript keeps a pet, a live chicken in a box.
He waits at the checkpoint; six months, then he's away.

3

Jerusalem

We hurry through arteries of crimson,
gold and spice, the souq's brave display,
into narrowing chambers; past cells
within cells, courtyards, closes, angles
where termite-pale families burrow deep
behind barred windows; down alleys
under the bulge of bloated buildings and out
on to a marble parade-ground bleached of life.

My companions wait patiently
for me to find out what it is I feel.
Not what I'm supposed to. The old slabs
glare in heartless sun. There's no more
than one or two souls, whispering to the Wall
like parted lovers, in a language
I don't speak. Scraps of paper prayer lodge
in dry-eyed crevices. But do they germinate?

To worship here would feel idolatrous.
There isn't the pretext of a Lady, weeping
plaster tears. This face is blank, unhaloed.
At our backs extends the seasick plaza,
swept bare of homes and mosques
in a surge of claustrophobia
prefiguring other acres bulldozed
for yet another wall, another wailing.

For this crazed Wall mimics the faultline
in my people, where the long hammering
of cruelty finally cracked us
and fear erupted. Many have since
built higher walls, bricked up

their emptied hearts in case of ambush.
They call them shrines. Like yours,
they hold the image of a broken-bodied Jew.

4

He said, *Just over that hill*
was the village of Deir Yassin.

History here speaks four languages.
Two are written on every roadsign:

The square-shouldered one stands above the other
which runs, throwing off diacritics like sweat.

Both are impenetrable to me, but I divine
that everything has two different names.

The third needs an interpreter, who remembers
what once lay over the silent sunbleached hill,

Who can explain the significance
of a tangled row of prickly pears

Who knows by what sleight the mighty Jordan
has been humbled to a runnel of poison-green.

But there is a fourth, written in concrete,
and even I can read these entrails fluently:

The rows of sharks' teeth gaping round the city,
the tarmac incisions that split the bloodless land.

5

The men in crisp shirts, the strategists, hold forth
in their seventh floor boardroom with its heavy table
of glass and blond wood, its commanding views.

A messy divorce, they comment drily,
domesticating Armageddon. When we say,
Tell us your grief, they only talk louder.

To meet the women, we must abandon pomp
for the clutter of an ordinary classroom. There
waits a plump kibbutznik, mother of six.

In schools, cafes, over garden walls, her neighbours
exchange bigotries. Armageddon lounges at her doorstep
calling her kids with the old lie. But she bars the way.

First one mother, one child, then another and another.
Without names or ranks or weapons or rosters
a *NO* is growing as big as an army.

6

Gaza

Down here in the sunstruck street
you can't see far – a wedge of sparkling sea,
stalls heaped with melons, corn, tomatoes
fat as moguls, traffic, coffee vendors,
shops, jacarandas, pestering barefoot boys
and sand in the gutters. The usual beach scene.

What can the kites see, straining as high
as their strings will let them? From above
the truth seems laid out plain as prison walls.
But hunger can't be seen from the sky. Or anger.
And the kites are stalled in a mockery of free air,
unable to see the gust coming from the future.

7

i.m. Mahmoud Darwish

She longs to go home.
As she passes, plantains
gawp and gossip, leaning their
tonsured heads close. She is ill;

it is possible she will die
without seeing her home, will be
buried in this alien soil –
her own, wrenched awry.

And if she could
cross, would home be palpable
under the concrete, the fir plantations,
the chlorine-eyed swimming pools?

Only the past
is familiar ground; only in dreams
do olives and almonds still flourish
where watchtowers now grow tall.

She is the Holy Land. She waits
to be claimed or disposed of
like an item of lost baggage
or a woman, where women are property.

Old as she is, she's a baby
in a chalk circle. She waits
for a Solomon
with the cunning, the power

the will to return her
where she belongs. Meanwhile, in her
ungentle foster-home, she waits,
struggling to keep the key.

My land

It was my first
ever moment of owning
real estate – a scrub field
and no bank, no landlord
standing between.

Surveying it, boom!
at once I was possessed
by possession, channelling
an Orwellian swine
of a laird

with a hundred thousand
acres... all that
expansiveness
that only makes the soul
contract. *My preciousss*

croaked the shrivelled
inner landowner, scowling
at tourists who looked over
the hedge, kids who jumped
the gate for their football.

I stalked
the seventy-eight paces
of *my* riverbank
under *my* trees, my shadow
lost in theirs:

the oaks growing since
before my grandparents
were born, the self-seeded
ash that would outlive
my grandchildren

while worms and nematodes
kept working, unseen, wordless.
Where were you
when we laid
the foundations of the earth?

As for me, I've made a start
on the ragwort and balsam,
planted more trees. The land
is mine – the way your mother is
or your muse.

Ness

A shipping container on stilts
  dumped on the seawall
or so it seemed
  from across three miles of marsh
in the February dusk. Inside
  all bright and shipshape, teatray
laid, scones and jam and Radio 4
  hobnobbing with the easy chairs.

Sand and shells give way
  to broken roof-shingles,
jigsawed wall-falls
  of London stock brick, tailfins
from a Zephyr. Bedded
  in black mud, the lumps
of concrete seem seachanged,
  sprouting tentacles of rebar.

On brackish fields wide
  as the sky, swans and clouds
nudge among the stubble. Brent geese
  black as stealth-bombers
scatter at the bittern-boom
  of artillery over at Foulness.
Skylarks and assault rifles
  trill canons together.

A flotsam of boxy dwellings
  at the water's edge I would say –
but it's all water, all edge.

No trees till St Osyth; bulrushes
morph into forest under the great blank.
The fishmonger (closed down)
offers 'muscles'. *Do not ask for credit*
as a smack in the mouth offen affends.

Icons

Vaideeni, Romania

It's a long way from gothic-gaunt
steeples meant to prod God
beyond reach. This one's
a gingerbread loaf. Colours
like a country fair, flocks of saints
up the walls, rugs, candlelight, grannies
in headscarves, golden syrup
of polyphonic chanting.

On their arthritic knees a whole morning,
they bow, cross, idolatrously kiss
the gilded lips of icons, crawl
under wooden reliquaries the shape
of old-fashioned kitchen cabinets
for a blessing. We Brits
last only an hour of repetition, glad
to escape into the sunlight.

Driving back, our host pulls up, calls over
a leather-skinned man in battered trilby.
Expecting a question, he comes close;
instead, a push sends him staggering
to loud guffaws. Our companions, warm,
hospitable, devout, pray for a Romania
without Roma, an icon with a gold border
to keep aloof the whole untamed steppe.

Cutting the line

I thought of walking round and round a space
Seamus Heaney

At Paddington, in the Tube
(Circle, eastbound) looking up at rain
through London's rusted ribs
I'm waiting for a ghost train.

Middle, Outer, Super-Outer – all
history. And Inner Circle's been twisted
into a paperclip. Today the trail
goes dead at Edgware Road.

London's all change, but
this breach doesn't augur
happiness: a wedding ring cut
from a swollen finger.

I mind the gap.
My inner baglady regrets
the last of the fixed orbits.
She's run her final lap

while sitting still, told her last beads.
There'll be no more decades
prayed on a golden rosary
coiled in the dark clay palm of the undercity.

My mystic mourns – for
without circumambulation
it's as if the Kaaba were no more
than a box round a black stone.

My ex-Londoner's rebelled.
They've ring-barked the great oak
though nothing was felled,
no drama or shock –

the painter quietly slips
unnoticed from the rail,
the Midgard serpent's tail
slides from slack lips.

I board the next train, catch
my doubled reflection, wonder
as always which
one of me isn't really there.

Fin de vacances

Nothing left but fingerprints
on mirrors, crumbs of playdough,
crashlanded storybooks, lone
socks, duvets stripped bare
and slumped on cold beds.

Now the house is hollow, a ribcage
that echoes to no small, clumping beat.
The kitchen clock drips like a tap.
Under the oak, two swings
beckon, out of sync.

The building is a gnomon.
A knife of shadow sweeps across –
each day in turn scythed down. At midday
the knife is deep in its heart.
But for the trees the sun would shrivel us.

The scallop shells on all the windowsills
look like conjoined feet
on a tomb effigy. Still, leaves
keep leaping, molehills erupt, and you
scoop a fledgling live from the water-butt.

Nothing but

They say
the sense of awe
can be induced
by stimulating a certain
part of the brain
with an electrode.
So that's awe
shown its place. As if it were nothing
that a feeble buzz of current
can shake open
the many-folded universe
inside 3lb of pink porridge.

Oh, we're ingenious:
our augmented eyes
take us deep into the ocean trenches
of our bodies: pulsing of colonic fins,
branched coral of milk-ducts. We can watch
an ammonite bud into humanity
but it's hammocked
in a life support system
way beyond human contrivance.
What looking-glass mother
will snort at her submariner
Why, you're nothing but a pack of cells!

Some fear knowledge
will gut mystery
like herring, bleed away
its potency. They fear the self-crowned
Lords of Nothing But. But
the real powerhouse
holds nothing
the mind can get a purchase on.

Go march into the Mandelbrot
labyrinth, and when
you've found the end
come back and tell us how you cracked
the walnut of infinity.

North

1 *Kallebua*

By night, by day, the sea ceaselessly
casts its great, green-blue nets
under mountains thin and hard
as salt cod, as fishing folk.
They have to be hard – that's how
they all survive, winter
after winter, so far north.

We laze where rowers slumped
exhausted in their snipe-legged
rorbuer, on bunks of board
high under stone shingle, turf or tin
while weather and labour
slowly shrivelled them, like stockfish
twisting on their gibbets.

Rorbu (pl. rorbuer) – shoreside wooden cabin for 'rowers', as Lofoten cod fishermen were known. Most of these cabins are now holiday homes.

2 *Å i Lofoten*

Awe is the word
as you arrive where
the one road simply
comes to a stop
and there's not even
a track or path onward
through the chaos of rocks
and rough ground.

You walk out
across hummocky turf
away from the campervan-
cluttered car park
into a skyful of quiet. Your eye
walks the spine of the cliff
to where the final vertebra
of the stegosaur's tail

dislimns in sunset. The last
abandoned hamlet is hidden
down there, and beyond
is nothing but sea –
orcas and deeps,
the Maelstrom, blue
legends, crosscurrents
to rip a rower's arms off.

3 *Öland*

For the solstice we've crossed
from Atlantic to Baltic,
to skin-and-bone fields
where people scratch a living
amid brindled herds
of limestone boulders.
This is the alvar.

The steeple's benign frown
has cowed the village dances
into whimsy. But the long stång
remembers a robuster time.
The meaning of the flowery O
that circles the heads of girls
in cags and wellies, is not quite lost.

Wherever life struggles
summer burns
the more intensely.
Low pink flames
tongue the alvar's hide,
the trees engorge,
bluefire runs wild along the shore.

(midsommar) stång – maypole decorated with greenery, used at Swedish midsummer celebrations

blå eld – 'blue fire', local name for wild lupin

Pilgrimage to Nevern

In the beginning, it's down
to the edge of the estuary.
No mystery here – everything
open, the land on its knees
to receive the tall blessing
of solstice. Then up the long hill,
Carn Ingli at our backs: an angel
defending us – or driving us out.

At the crest, we must turn aside,
cross the stile that leads out of the sun
and under the shadow of trees. Deeper
in gloom we cross the mossy stones
hand in hand, our feet slipping.
Past the pilgrim's cross, scratched
on a rockface, half-hidden; until at last
we glimpse the church steeple.

The empty little streets are shining
in the clean light – the whole village
still, as if praying. Even
the rooks are listening
to the silence. The yew's tears,
the Ogham, the wormtrails
etched in stone, speak an ancient tongue
we'll never quite understand.

The veil between the worlds

i.m. Waldo Williams 1904-1971

At Millin Cross there is a church
where you came, once, at turn of night
hoping to see the veil between
the worlds dissolve, if you timed it right.

On tiptoe, I peer through the windows,
but catch no glimmer of your presence,
just pews, altar, slanting light.
I listen a long while to the silence.

Down the hill the crooked oak
still stands at the edge of the great basin
where two rivers flow together
and the sea runs up to meet them.

You saw the King among the rushes;
you sensed the sun beyond the sun,
eternity in your neighbours reaping –
no veil between the two worlds then.

The dust-motes glinting in the chapel air,
the leaves whispering all along the lane,
the water's expanse held shining in the branches,
the moment of blessing in a world aflame

all seem to say: There is another world
but it is this one.

Where are we going?

We are squanderers of sorrows.
How we peer ahead into their sad duration
to see if maybe they will end.

R M Rilke

New Monkey
Lesula (Cercopithecus lomamiensis) identified as a new species by scientists in 2012

Not that you are – only new
to us Westerners, know-alls of the planet.
You look as if you've been around
a long, long time. (And so you have,
millions more years than the new apes
on the block.) But also as if
you'd seen us coming.

Not that we should be tempted
to think we can read your soul, just because
you look like an old geezer who's just
been dragged out of a cellar, with your
long grubby beard, lugubrious nose, lips
pressed between apologetic smile
and fear of what's coming.

Not that you know, though you certainly
kept a low profile – *shy and quiet*
the description. But they've pinned you down
just in time, given you a fancy name
before you disappear, following
all the rest into the crammed
cattlecars that keep on coming.

Not that we're entitled to see
ourselves looking back
out of your shadowed eyes, old man
of the woods. Compared to you
we're babies – we take
being fed for granted, still believe in milk
not in what's coming.

Whether

1

For an hour
    we've hired the experience
of life in the marais:
    low in the water,
half-submerged, nearly dissolved
    in liquid light
squatting on hard boards
    in the fisherman's punt
towered over
    by forests of osiers where
hunters hide; and out
    on to the levels of shining
water, where time slows
    to the almost subliminal
flow of the current, and sound
    lulls down to the hush
of breeze in reeds, the small lapping
    of our wake against the piles,
creak of wood, quiet comments
    from passing wildfowl.
Even the marais' words
    whisper: *roseaux,*
chaume, chaland, sangsue.

But when Madame
    in her curlers lifts the dripping
punt-pole over our shoulders
    to point out
with an alarming dip of the boat
    a goose or grazing cow
as if they were rarities, then
    a distant steeple-tip –

the only building
    visible, thanks to
its six-metre elevation –
    I foresense
        the drowned future
we are drifting dreamily towards.

2

Bleached hillsides are crawling
back out of the reservoirs
stratum by stratum. Empty
window sockets stare wave-lidded
from the skulls of dead villages.
And I'm wondering, dry?

Already it's high noon
on the high seas, the showdown
imminent between glacier
melt and the outnumbered
Gulf Stream. So, cold, then?

... Do not forsake me O my darling ...

There is such confusion
in the woods: November
daffodils, bluebells at Easter,
insomniac squirrels, buds
among the berries. So maybe, hot?

... You are lost and gone forever ...

But what about last week –
the whole sky possessed
by sheet lightning, and us
driven to a standstill by cataracts
of rain, over the feeble protest
of the wipers.   Flood?

And I'm wondering: of your grandchildren
and mine, just now playing football
so heedlessly in the invisible
haze of exhaust – who
will make it to an overcrowded Ararat?

Will ye go, lassie, go? and we'll all go together...

3

"A process in the weather of the heart" – installation by Angharad Taris

What are they? cutlasses
facing off, rust-eaten as Tybalt's
quarrel, temper still dangerous,
mouldered as tyrants in their vaults.

Screw-holes bored
in the greater of the two suggests a hinge.
A locked exit could
explain the other's cringe.

Shards of fuselage:
vestigial clue
to a mid-air barrage
that vaporised the crew?

Or hull-plates dredged
from the toxic scurf
that was once the Aral Sea; left edge
a harsh horizon; right a fossil surf.

Rat-bitten
slabs of salt cod, their iridescence
long dulled to a crust of dead chitin
the colour of old underpants.

Excavated scene
depicting some ancient funeral rite?
This last king and queen
ride away into devouring light.

Violent isotopes that emit
unseen rays, decaying to a standoff.
How many centuries is the half-life
of hate?

Mildew, acid, bacteria, spores
are busy making the world anew
in curd-white, russet, penicillin-blue.
Some day, all this will be theirs.

Mass for the Oort cloud

Introit: Inside the Large Hadron Collider

'Twas a dark and stormy night
and the captain turned to Higgs boson
and said, *Bos'n, tell us a story.*

So the boson began:
'Twas a dark and stormy night
and the captain turned to Higgs boson
and said, *Bos'n, tell us a story.*

So the boson began ...

*

Credo

though photons have no mass
while neutrinos
have mass but
no charge. And out there
dark masses
that no-one
can account for.
I believe
in the God particle
quia impossibile est.

*

Benedictus

What we can observe
is nothing;
most of what there is is

inference, labelled
by stabs in the dark: dark
energy   dark matter.
Blackbodies: *idealised*
physical beings that absorb
all incident (are we
talking angels?).
Lucky us, part
of the four per cent
that is seen.
And of the
who knows what
per cent
that also sees.

*

Agnus dei

Thar she blows!
telltale trace
on the horizon. No
leviathan – behold
the speck of god-dust
that takes away
the weight
of that mighty
unaccounted for
dark mass
(well, maybe). Load
it up with all
your unanswered
questions, scientists!
If only
it could take
away our own

darkness – but
even if we
conscientiously put out
our garbage, there's
no celestial dustcart
to call; and
where
could it be taken?
Out in that desert
no benign
kites and gulls
wait.

*

Sanctus

The heavens
are full
of
– what?
Shall we say
glory
dark
immeasurable
as the coast
of Britain?

*

Gloria

Oh, these shoals
of dazzling minnows
that keep slipping through
the solar-flung net
of the Oort cloud

a light-year out,
beyond Neptune
in the highest –
meaning the furthest
shore of our sun's
fishing-ground.

*

Dies irae

No-one
has ever observed
the Oort cloud
or knows for sure
it's there. Or whether
it will one day
rise up
leave its nets and follow
the call
of Proxima Centauri
as it comes walking
over the interstellar waves.
Or what will
happen next.

*

Kyrie eleison.

Benoît('Blessed') Mandelbrot wrote a paper in 1967 called How long is the coast of Britain?, which launched the concept of fractal geometry. He later suggested that the darkness of the night sky (the Olbers' paradox) could be accounted for by fractal distribution of stars.

Sunbrick burial ground

A ewe with her lamb, that fled
as we came in, hovers at the entrance
scratching her backside on the jamb
as she waits for us to leave.

Not that the grass in here is any richer
for the dust beneath. After all those centuries
there can't be much virtue remaining
from two hundred buried Quakers.

A straggle of trees round the boundary
form the honour guard: one nipped hawthorn
holding back its blossom, a half-dozen
unsentimental ash like old soldiers

brutally barbered by the wind,
easing tired backs out of the rock, dangling
fag-ends of bud – and one field maple
flaunting tassels and fluorescent green.

She'd have liked that, old Margaret Fox,
who loved brave colours
and scorned the uniform of Quaker grey –
a silly, poor Gospel:

It's the spirit inside that counts.
She probably wouldn't
have minded that the inscription
chiselled on a boulder

is already half obliterated, or
that some far-off day
all sign of human presence
will have been wiped.

So we walk up to the trig-point, up
into today's May weather and the big clean sky,
above the burial ground and the stone circle
and the Morecambe mud-flats.

High above the golf course and the chemical works,
above the nuclear power station, above
the stark-white wind turbines we take our stand
with larks and limestone and nibbled turf.

Margaret Fox, the 'mother' of the Quaker movement, is buried at Sunbrick on Birkrigg Common in Cumbria

Everything is illuminated

"Not to be used for glasswear" – sign on bin at doctor's surgery

Well, why not? What could be more apt
than to decant our watery selves
into tumblers? Picture it:

Catwalks where supermodels strut, breasts
flaunting high voltage insulators. And for men:
codpieces of magnifying glass.

The brassy would go about in plate-glass. The modest
would plump for strategic frosting or drape
chandeliers about their loins to refract prying eyes.

Picture us in fish scales, champagne flutes, lava-lamps.
Or windows software for comfort. Naughty kids would stand
at road junctions flashing red, amber, green.

Picture the weddings: older guests solemn
in stained-glass, young ones wired for instant
communication in their optic fibre gear.

The bride meanwhile would be an opaque vision
in moulded fibreglass. Jewish bridegrooms
would simply click their ankles for good luck....

Suits of obsidian would be de rigueur
in the City, outside nightclubs or
wherever else hard men are to be found.

How careful we'd have to be! The fairskinned
might need whole-body mirrored shades;
perspex or plexi for butterfingers or children.

And where to stash our wallet, cards,
I-stuff? Smash-and-grab could get personal.
Keep dusting for fingerprints.

We'd all need to be gentler, slower-moving,
for fear of tears and tears.
No-one would throw stones.

Massif

Beech forests
    have superb PR.
Because they build such lofty columns
    of still air; because it is cool
and hushed in there; because
    sometimes you glimpse
a vast blue strath beyond;
    because year on year
the charred sheaves they shed
    pile up at their feet
like concertina files
    of the disappeared – leaves
so compacted by time
    that waterfalls carve them
as if they were rock strata –

because all this quiets you, you
    mistake your own caught breath
for eternity.   But look
    here, how the earth has slumped
away from under roots,
    how these titans have dumped
the odd limb with no more
    ceremony than a lizard.
Look at the boulders –
    ten-ton knucklebones
left teetering
    halfway down the scarp, detained
for now by a single branch,
    or balanced impossibly, one stone
coprolite atop another.

The plateau makes no such
    tall claims. Stripped down
for the long haul, it grits
    granite teeth against the weather.
Ground-angels nail themselves
    to meagre soil: stonecrop
and viola don't go in for soaring,
    they're not above
all that mortality stuff.
    Seizing the moment
broom combusts everywhere.
    Wild tulips whisper the message
from parched throats streaked
    with scarlet:
This year we made it.

Arachnophilia

I've begun to notice their uncanny
powers: the gift of flight
without wings, angelic
basejumping
on a single filament
so fine it is almost nothingness.

The knack of invisibility – think
of those dawn walks
when you blunder face-first into
a booby-trap from Lilliput. (Only mist,
hiding all else, blows their cover
with diamonds.)

And superhuman strength –
a screen of gossamer
could stop a jet at full throttle. Hey,
how about an arachnid bullet-proof vest?
The bullet would bounce back, oh yes....
after travelling fifteen more inches.

No lab-coated Penelope has ever
woven spider-silk. But once
someone took a spider into space
by accident. For two days
the patterns were chaotic, but on the third
behold! a perfect orb-web.

So I try to choke back
my conditioned shudder
and learn to value spiders.
Once we've done our worst, maybe
they'll be among the ones
who will reweave this jangled Ithaca.

Now we are sixty

I'm naked in the mirror. No horses
frightened yet – smooth flesh,
clear eyes, breasts small enough
to outface gravity, waist a little
thickened, badger hair
still more dark than grey.

It's a cover-up. You can't see
the crone bits: crabbed joints,
blown eggs, the hideyholes
where skin is thinned
like rotted silk. My secret: I'm
juiceless. I mourn dead delight.

The muse arrives – not the usual
sullen teenager, away
night after night, coming home only
to snub me. This time
he's a satyr: bearded, hairy-arsed,
unpredictable as a billygoat.

He laughs at me, not unkindly,
takes my hand, leads me
out into fields whose moist breath
is tinged with wild honeysuckle
and slurry. I hear the willow
warbler's long shudder,

get stoned on sweet honesty,
the piña colada of gorse, feel resin rise
in gnarled cypresses. He puts an apple
into my hand – I crunch with the teeth
of imagination – so much more
hardwearing than real enamel.

And so to bed, on my birthday night
the just-past-full moon revving west
headlamp on high beam.

Leaving

It's February, but no lambs will come
to these small fields, blotched
with a psoriasis of reeds and thistles.

It began gradually. The post office
closed, then the school. The young people
went away for work. The older ones died out.

Now the neat houses are deserted,
chapel boarded up, outlines
of garden beds blurred.

The last straggler stays on
too vague and frail to patch up the leaks
or notice the rotting window frames.

It won't be long before his roof collapses.
Hazel and ash will move in, buddleia
kindle in the cold hearth.

This is one way of describing the ruin
of old Doug, shuffling behind his cobwebs
amid the cheery pastels of the care home.

He knows there are proprieties, stands up
again and again, picks frowning at a stain
on his trousers. Begins politely, *I'm afraid*

Heart of oak

The sturdy trunk gaped unexpectedly:
a bothy of bark. In the triangular
opening, imagine a hermit
living on nothing, dispensing oracles.

I kept a respectful distance, didn't gawp
inside, taking at face value
the massy corona of boughs,
brocade of leaf, a weight upheld of old.

Next time I passed, I had company.
Have you looked inside? he said.
I stuck my head in, twisted my neck
squinted up, saw sky.

This oak is just a loo-roll tube!
not throne, not anchorhold, not even timber.
The crown is hollow. From further off
bare jagged bones on top are obvious.

Yet I wasn't all wrong: the shell supports
a weight of life, its own and colonies
of fungi, grubs, beetles. Song-birds
entrust it with their broods.

Extraordinary, that gift
of trust still being freely bestowed
to the last, and even by some
who've seen the emptiness inside.

Cloud walking

First experience of Qigong

Your bare left foot kisses the grass goodbye
and rises ten thousand feet
into sunshine and silence. Far below
traffic still drones, birds chatter,
time still runs too fast.

Your upturned sole advances, proud
as a Zulu warrior; your raised right palm
holds no assegai but declares: *Stop!*
Make way: this footfall belongs to ME.
A gilded insect validates the triumph.

But now your heel sinks tenderly
into the shivery dew, a softened hand
lowers with utmost care through
the rarefied air, trying not to
wake it from its baby-sleep.

Meanwhile, right foot, left hand
have begun their journey to claim
the next yard of experience.
You are dignified and daft
as a hen. You can be here any time.

Indigo Dreams Publishing Ltd
24, Forest Houses
Cookworthy Moor
Halwill
Beaworthy
Devon
EX21 5UU
www.indigodreams.co.uk